D1550936

The People of CHINA

Lynn M. Stone

The Rourke Book Company, Inc.
Vero Beach, Florida 32964

PHOTO CREDITS
© Keren Su: title page, p. 4, 7, 8, 13, 15, 17, 21;
© Lynn M. Stone: p. 10, 12, 18

Library of Congress Cataloging-in-Publication Data

Stone, Lynn M.
    The people of China / Lynn M. Stone.
        p. cm. — (China)
    Includes index.
    ISBN 1-55916-319-4
    1. China—Juvenile literature. [1. China] I. Title.

DS706 .S795 2000
951—dc21
                                                        00–038725

Printed in the USA

CONTENTS

THE PEOPLE OF CHINA

China has more people than any other other country. More than 1 billion people live in China. Each year China adds about 15 million people. That is about equal to the entire population of Australia!

Most Chinese people live in the eastern one-third of the nation. Most of the largest cities, like Shanghai and Beijing, are in the east. Most of the country's best farmland is there, too.

In colorful slickers, bicyclists on their way to work wait for a traffic light on a rainy morning in Shanghai.

China has about 40 cities with 1 million or more people. The largest is Shanghai with more than 8 million.

About three of every four Chinese people, however, live in **rural**, or outlying, villages. And about 7 of every 10 Chinese workers have farm jobs.

One of China's biggest problems is trying to provide a good life for its huge **population**.

The Chinese New Year is always cause for music, fairs, parades, and the lion dance seen here in Beijing.

CHINESE CULTURE

China has the oldest living **culture** on earth. The Chinese even have a written history dating back 3,500 years. Compare that to the age of the United States, which officially began in 1776!

The Chinese were the first to make paper. They were also the first to develop the compass, make silk cloth, and use **porcelain**.

A fair brings people to the streets of Nanjing in Jiangsu Province.

The largest group of people in China are the Han. Almost 92 of every 100 people in China belong to the Han group.

The Han speak Chinese, but the language has several forms called **dialects**. Different groups pronounce words differently, but they write Chinese the same way.

The Chinese alphabet uses marks known as characters instead of the alphabet you know. Each Chinese character is a **symbol**. The character can stand for a whole word or part of a word.

Chinese characters appear on signs by a small shop in Sichuan Province.

Strollers spend a sunny Sunday afternoon along Shanghai's waterfront.

Rice terraces are like giant steps on this hillside in Longi, Guangxi Province.

13

CHINESE MINORITIES

China is the third-largest country in area. It is slightly bigger than the United States and smaller than only Russia and Canada.

Within China's broad borders live some 56 **minorities**. Minorities are groups of people that are fewer in number than a country's main group, such as China's Han. Minority groups in China include Kazakhs, Mongols, Tibetans, and Uigurs, among others. Most of the minority groups have their own language and culture.

A boy of the Tibetan minority in China sits atop a woolly yak in Shigatse, Tibet.

LIFE IN CHINA

China is rapidly becoming more modern. But many jobs in China are still done in old-fashioned ways. For instance, animals, instead of machines, are often used for farm work. Crops are often planted and harvested by hand.

By **Western** ways of measuring, China is still a poor country. It doesn't have nearly as many machines, computers, or vehicles as Western countries like Canada and the United States.

Workers plant rice seedlings by hand in Guizhou Province.

Nearly all adults in China work. Most people in rural areas raise farm crops. They make little money, but they have plenty of food and clothing. They live in small houses of mud and bricks or stone.

Urban, or city, people make more money. Most city people live in apartment buildings. China's urban people can often afford motorbikes and televisions. Few people own cars.

Urban Chinese live in apartment buildings where the central government keeps rent prices low.

THE CHINESE GOVERNMENT

The people of China live under a powerful central government run by the Communist party. The government helps keep the cost of food, clothing, housing, and medicine low. But China's style of government is much more controlling of people's lives than the governments of the West. For example, the government owns most factories, banks, and transport systems in China.

The central government controls education, too. Students begin school at the age of 6 or 7. They must attend school for at least 6 years.

The Chinese government organizes many student groups and activities, including this group that promotes clean streets.

CHINESE PRODUCTS

Chinese farmers generally must work with simple tools and hand labor. But Chinese farms turn out a great variety of crops. These include rice, cabbage, cotton, corn, peanuts, wheat, tea, and soybeans.

China has rich natural resources. It has a major fishing industry and plenty of coal, oil, slate, tin, copper, and other materials.

Chinese factories produce great amounts of cement, chemicals, clothing, machines, iron, and steel.

GLOSSARY

culture (KUL chur) — the special ways in which a certain group of people live; the beliefs, customs, language, and other characteristics of a group

dialect (DIE uh lekt) — within a single language, a different variety of that language

minority (muh NAWR uh tee) — a small group within a much larger one

population (pah pyoo LAY shun) — the total number of people living in a place

porcelain (PAWR suh lun) — a hard, shiny type of ceramic created from baked white clay and other raw materials

rural (RER ul) — of the country

symbol (SIM bul) — that which stands for something else, like a flag being a symbol of a nation

urban (UR bun) — of the city

Western (WES tern) — of the Western part of the world, including the Americas and Western Europe

FURTHER INFORMATION

Find out more about the people of China and China in general with these helpful books and information sites:

- King, D and Parker, L. *Dropping in on China.* Rourke, 1998
- Maywan, Shen Krach. *D is for Doufu: A Book of Chinese Culture.* Shen's Books, 1997
- Stephens, Keeler. *Passport to China.* Franklin Watts, 1997
- Williams, Suzanne. *Made in China: Ideas and Inventions from Ancient China.* Pacific View, 1997
China on-line at www.mytravelguide.com
Lonely Planet-Destination China on-line at www.lonelyplanet.com

INDEX